waterways poetry

Plums

releasing new voices, revealing new perspectives

Plums
published by the waterways series, 2011
a contemporary poetry series of flipped eye publishing

First Edition
Copyright © Kate McLoughlin, 2011
Front Image: Pablo Picasso, *Las Meninas, Conjunto, 1957* © Succession Picasso/
DACS, London 2011. Photograph provided by Museu Picasso de Barcelona.
Rear Image: Diego Velázquez, *Las Meninas*, 1656
Cover Design © Petraski, flipped eye publishing, 2011

ISBN-10: 1-905233-34-5
ISBN-13: 978-1-905233-34-2

British Library Cataloguing in Publication Data
A catalogue record for this book is available from the British Library

Editorial work for this book was supported by the Arts Council of England

LOTTERY FUNDED

In memory of my grandmother, Hilda Shipman (1896-1998)

Plums

Kate McLoughlin
2011

Acknowledgements

With thanks to Nick Trefethen and Nii Ayikwei Parkes, as well as the many rights holders who have helped facilitate the production of this book.

Plums

Variations on William Carlos Williams' *This Is Just To Say*
after Pablo Picasso's *Las Meninas*

This Is Just To Say

I have eaten
the plums
that were in
the icebox

and which
you were probably
saving
for breakfast

Forgive me
they were delicious
so sweet
and so cold

(William Carlos Williams, 1934)

i

Those plums
you took from the icebox
I was saving them for breakfast

I tore
up your note

ii

Those plums you
took from the icebox
I was saving them for breakfast

So sorry
I should have picked enough for two

iii

Those plums you took from the icebox
I was saving them for breakfast
But you left before dawn
Eat them with my love.

iv

Those plums you took from
the icebox: I was saving
them for breakfast

While the world reads your note,
what will I have?

v

Those plums you took
from the icebox
I was saving them for breakfast

They are the last things you'll take of mine.

vi

My plums, my plums,
Purple-biding, brooding,
Bruise-purple,
A sheen shining on
My purple beauties
Cloistered in my jewel-box
My clutch of amethyst eggs.

vii

O O O my plums!
You have breached and bruised them
Gorged on them
Wolfed them
Sucked and smacked your lips
Their juice runs down your chin.

viii

plums – icebox
sweet – cold

purple – gold

ix

you – I
forgive

x

you I
still dance

xi

delicious (purplegold)

xii

so cold the icebox
sweet you have probably just eaten the plums that were in
for breakfast
which were
and they were
delicious
and This is to say I Forgive
saving me so

xiii

Not just but unjust

cold/hot sweet/sour
doesn't matter
save/splurge irrelevant

Not just but unjust

xiv

       plums   plums   plums
plums   plums   plums
forgive me forgive me forgive me forgive me
sweet delicious cold sweet delicious cold
icebox   icebox   icebox
       icebox   icebox   icebox

At the heart of the rose
The hub of the hive
Deep in the ice
Sweetness lies.

You broke through the ice
Stole out the plum
Will the rose and the hive
So swiftly succumb?

Nectar and honey
Crimson joy
O rose thou art lost
I am sick, I must die.

xvi

Plums? What plums?
Oh no, I wasn't saving those.
Don't you yet know
I don't like fruit?

xvii

This is just to say

I took the red wheelbarrow
That you depend upon so much

I wiped off the rain
It's starting to rust

xviii

No, it was not for breakfast I was saving them
But for a picnic I thought we'd share
In the woods above the house
Where the sun spears the leaves
I thought we'd lie together, sticky, full of plums,
Drunk on the icy water of the stream.

xix

I see you reaching into the ice
A fisherman reeling out his line through a hole in the frozen lake.

xx

The drawer of my desk is open
My book of poems gone
I pick up what now lies there:
On my palm a plum.

xxi

Better to remember them ripening,
Clustered, pendent from the tree
(remember the blossom of the plumtree?)
The sun dusting tight skins with light
Fat purple drips
Aching to drop

xxii

green
indigo

xxiii

They fall late
That are sweetest
Plummet into our lives
Changing things

xxiv

Burst bodies
Torn skin
Red and yellow matter
Spatters floor and wall

xxv

This Is Just
To Say

I have steamed open your envelopes
Traced the letters on your writing pad

I have read your diaries
Yes, even the locked diary

I have winkled out your password
Hacked into your email

I know about last Tuesday

As you despoiled plums
I plumbed your depths

xxvi

This Is Just Touché

I have stolen
the identity
that you had constructed

and which
you were probably
keeping forever

Forgive me
it was exciting
so vast
and so you

xxvii

Diego Velázquez
canvases
window
light fittings

Doña Agustina de Sarmiento de Sotomayor - Doña Margarita Theresa
    de España -
Doña Isabel de Velasco - Maribárbola - Nicolasito Pertusato - Dog

Philip IV of Spain / Mariana of Austria (mirror) - Don José Nieto de
    Velázquez
(open door) - Doña Marcela de Ulloa - Guard

I - plums - you
forgive - saving
delicious - sweet - cold
icebox - breakfast

xviii

Reflections in the window
A turned back, a grasping hand

xxix

Yes, someone watched you, helping yourself
Did you not know the door was open?
Did you not see the window ajar
and the lights, the blazing lights?
Did you not smell the rank dog or
hear the rasp of his panting jaws?

xxx

You slipped in at daybreak
I was sleeping

xxxi

It was night
The sour smell of the woodshed numbed by the cold
A dark snack, a midnight feast
Did you snigger, slightly, at the sweetness?

xxxii

Embryos in the freezer
Unimplanted

xxxiii

I
plums
icebox
you
breakfast
forgive
delicious
sweet
cold
sweet
delicious
forgive
breakfast
you
icebox
plums
I

xxxiv

saving forgive

xxxv

'This is just to say' says so much
Holds out such promise:
The plumtree in blossom
Ice forming in the water
You and I starting out

xxxvi

Frozen so they would not wither
Icebox imagism.

xxxvii

just
plums

xxxviii

Would you return
to the moment
when you stretched out your hand?

xxxix

Actually I heard you sucking them.
It was disgusting
I ran to get away.

And again the next day
When the sweet fumes of their rotting
Filled the warm air.

xl

Saving
Yes, I was saving those fallen plums.

xli

Did you discover them by chance, searching for something else,
only realise, too late, I was keeping them for breakfast?

Or did you watch me place them there, guess my purpose,
act to thwart my desire?

xlii

How all our lives had brought us to that point,
All that we did and were culminated
In 'I will pick plums for breakfast',
'I will open the icebox'.
Two outstretched arms – to pick, to pluck –
So nearly found each other, yet
Though the trajectories came close, failed to meet,
And so sailed onwards undiverted,
Leaving as the only sign of our want of coincidence
A quarrel over plums.

xliii

I didn't pick them
Neither did they fall.
I bought them on special offer
Down at the market stall.

xliv

Plump presumptuous plums
Ripe for crushing.

xlv

When I published his note
I was not expecting this attention.
He meant nothing by it.
He knows he need not seek my forgiveness
Nor speak of sweet and cold.

xlvi

The fierceness of your need
Is alien.
How can I forgive
What I don't understand?

xlvii

Like Velázquez, you look out from your work
Depict yourself in the act of depicting,
Your addressees, like his subjects,
Are known and unknown.
But 'Forgive me' suggests you see
That figure on the threshold
Breathing over your shoulder
Bearing your own name.

xlviii

Picasso's dog sniffs the plums
A few black brushstrokes
Purple

xlix

In deep ocean
Ancient sea-snails
The murex, discharging dye
For Emperors' togas.
Royal purple.

l

This Is Just To Say

I published
the note
I found on
the icebox

and which you probably dashed
off in
a hurry

Forgive me
I did not realise
what I
had done.

li

Refrigeration merely extends our opportunities
For stealing fruit.
How far we have come!

lii

First
we did not need to talk.
Now
we cannot.
Notes
flutter vainly between us.

liii

Have they enlightened you
Those plums of knowledge
You fell over yourself to eat?

Did they taste good?

liv

If I try to explain why I mind
You won't hear it.
You'll hear recrimination,
Think yourself criticised.
Better not to speak?
Let the silence congeal around us?
I might as well live in the icebox
Yet how can I live without you?

lv

The moment before I found the note
Before I understood
The first disobedience.

lvi

The Habsburgs have come to New Jersey
Here is their entourage:
Meninas, dwarves, the royal hound,
Chaperones, guards, the Queen's Chamberlain
And naturally the court painter, Diego Rodríguez de Silva y Velázquez
And another painter, short, irascible,
With a surprisingly long name -
Pablo Diego José Francisco de Paula Juan Nepomuceno María de los
    Remedios Cipriano de la Santísima Trinidad Ruiz y Picasso,
Preening his plumage, PP has invited
Francis Bacon and his screaming popes
(who know Velázquez well),
And that means Mark-Anthony Turnage
Who is carrying on ice Dylan's pyramids,
Heaney's Bog People and the local plumber (a lead weight),
Little Jack Horner has thumbed a lift
With Charles Bukowski (who should wash his mouth out),
The writer of Genesis and Milton are in the retinue
(yes, an English Protestant accompanies these Spanish Catholics,
and so why not the theologians of free will and predestination,
the Reformers and Counter-Reformers? Luther will eat plum pie),
And there are the poets of corruption, Nashe and Blake,
And in the far distance, Larkin, who knows a little of forbidden fruit.
Red wheelbarrows, white chickens and roses
Clutter up the hallways,
Here is Marianne Moore, real toads in tow,
And H.D., *Imagiste* (her nom-de-plume),
Ezra Pound was not invited –
He can go smear arsenic on his

lvii

The saying is all
Not the plums
But the penning:
The writing endures
Words continue
At the heart of us: a text.

lviii

Now, with aplomb
Let us join hands
And dance around
The icebox
The complex minuet
We have perfected
These long years
The well-worn steps
A testament
To our mutual comfort
And yes
Our mutual trust.

A Plumentary

I and *you* are the poles of the poem's main axis. They create a forcefield;
all else depends on them. *Plums* and *icebox* form another, weaker axis.
Breakfast doesn't really matter. *Forgive* orbits above; *delicious, sweet* and
cold are satellites circling in their own orbit. (*Saving* is more significant
than it initially seems.) In his 58-painting series, *Las Meninas* (1957), on
display in Barcelona, Picasso opened and closed the window on Diego
Velázquez's *Las Meninas* (1656). 301 years after Velázquez's original,
Side Window changes the lighting (the *light fittings* are seldom omitted).
The *dresses* must be triangular, the *Court Chamberlain* is always at the
half-open door. But the painter vanishes and sometimes the scene is
changed entirely: a balcony over the sea at Cannes, a stranger at the
piano. And the royal hound is *Dog*: four legs, two ears, snout and tail.

Thank you for buying *Plums*. It is Kate McLoughlin's first poetry collection. She has also published non-fiction in the field of war writing. You can find out more about her at:
http://bit.ly/FE_author_kate

—§—

the waterways series is an imprint of flipped eye publishing, a small publisher dedicated to publishing powerful new voices in affordable volumes. Founded in 2001, we have won awards and international recognition through our focus on publishing fiction and poetry that is clear and true, rather than exhibitionist.

If you would like more information about flipped eye publishing, please join our mailing list online at **www.flippedeye.net**.

Lightning Source UK Ltd.
Milton Keynes UK
UKOW051417110112

185178UK00003B/20/P